I0087505

Aquilegia

♣

Venomous Verses

Aquilegia

Venomous Verses

Rosaria Trenta

CANISTRIGGER

PUBLISHING

This book is fully protected by copyright.
© CanisTrigger Publishing

AQUILEGIA (VENOMOUS VERSES).
Copyright © 2011 by Rosaria Trenta.

All rights reserved. No part of this book may be used or reproduced in any manner whatsoever without written permission except in the case of brief quotations embodied in critical articles and reviews. For information address CanisTrigger Publishing, Södra Esplanaden 22, SE-275 75 Lövestad, Sweden.

All characters in this publication are fictitious and any resemblance to real persons, living or dead, is purely coincidental.

Trade Paperback ISBN: 978-91-978707-1-9

Printed and bound by
Lightning Source Inc.

Visit us on the web at www.canistriggerpublishing.com

Original cover design by CanisTrigger Publishing

To all my torturers

Contents

Le dragon rugit encore . . .

Foreword

*A*quilegia, the beautiful garden flower, is also known as the symbol of folly and lost love. Rosaria Trenta has poignantly used its symbolism to epitomise the folly of feelings and their excesses of emotions. Her poetry reflects her struggles with loss and despair, and we entirely understand such feelings; indeed, we sympathise with them, because we also have anguished over abandonment and loss. There is honesty and sharpness in the verses, as venomous as the *Aquilegia* seeds when grounded up in wine. This is a riveting read, unflinching and full of pathos.

Plato wrote that 'a man must first know the truth about every single subject on which he speaks or writes'. In Rosaria Trenta's work her poetic sensitivity transpires in the way she brutally exposes her soul, coming down to the nitty-gritty when it calls for showing feelings for what they are. Alas, there are no half measures, no sugar-coated truth: the soil is fertile for a suffering soul to lay bare the most intimate pain and discomfort.

The *Aquilegia* seeds—so deeply planted— are destined to bloom, and perhaps the temptation to contemplate the beauty of nature is strong; yet, the author presents a cogent argument that her condition reflects the solitary state of her life, deprived of some vital elements. Such a confinement inevitably erupts in the lyrical dimension of the poetic space, becoming both friend and foe, in a constant attempt to re-establish a connection with her own familiar world. But the emptiness inside is only apparent and there is much more than a lifeless void, though a latent fear of rejection is present.

The author might ultimately overcome her sentiments of sadness and anxiety, leaving behind a feeling of dismally low spirits once this cathartic exercise reaches its conclusion through a symbolic death. The doleful time is past: now is the winter of our discontent.

Esme Mann

[1] Debt of nature.

I Die

Spare me from this torture,
the fatal rapture
of a deadly mistake.

The hands of time
are never fine:
past dreams are over.

What would I be
without the shattered me?
My body rots in hell.

No friend or foe,
I've sunk so low.
Damnation my fate.

And so down I go,
farewell and adieu!
Tainted dirty soul:
I die.

Lament

I don't care that you ignore me
I don't mind that you forget me.
You touched my soul
And it flew away,
You messed with my heart
And it went astray.

Forsaken perhaps recoiled
In the fretful mind that never sleeps;
Imagined and strongly desired
In the perpetual silence of death
That hurts so deep.

You can't see me in the shadow
You won't hear me in the dark;
I kissed your lips
And they dried my sorrow,
I smacked your cheek
And it filled with colour.

I don't care if you destroy me
I don't mind if you reject me.
We have sinned, despised and cursed,
We left nothing untouched, unheard.
Too late for questions, no reason to repent:
We frugally dispense the grains of time.

No cheating spouse to gracefully resent
The shattered heart that we cannot mend
Confined to a rhyme in this devil's lament.

Disconnected

I'm paraphrasing, rearranging
my words that choke on nothing,
stuck in his voracious mouth.
An abyss engulfing tears and laughter
at the same pace and speed
of the diagonal thought,
the subversive dimension
where we both met.

Once there was my hope,
it went out to find him
and returned empty-handed.
The syllables vacuously spoken,
so I grabbed his smile
and made it mine;
trapped it forever within a circle of ruins,
buried under tons of garbage
and rotting corpses deprived of life,
slowly turning into empty carcasses.

I possessed him for a moment,
before he slipped away
tenaciously sought after
by a hundred more spiteful souls.
And they never questioned,
they never pulled back;
whatever he asked for they gave,

driven by their insatiable hunger
for his dire manly needs.

Who am I?
What is this thing that burns without flames?
Repulsive fiend, mere illusion,
but every time I fall
it's there to catch me:
won't let me die,
won't let me live.
His face ridicules my defeat,
the ashes scattered in the wind
blowing into our face,
as we grab each other's soul
and say: 'It's time to go. It's time
to let go.'

What am I?
Who is he?
The fearsome liar,
the image of a demon,
a stale memory
in the daily stampede
I want out of.
And sublimation of his ominous intent
is ultimately fake,
like all things immaterial
in this total vacuum cell.

We said it aloud
though it doesn't matter.
This life was meant to end

livid and vengeful,
scarred in many ways,
rebuilt on sandy pillars,
dissected and distorted,
forgotten and unwanted.
Yet I want him
to see my true intentions,
can't have my identity mistaken,
my wish savagely rejected.
I don't want to be invisible,
I'm not going to be dis-con-nect-ed.

DONE!

Paralysed
Ostracised
Dying here
Dead already
Gone, gone, gone

Lobotomised
Interiorised
Crying here
All cried out
Killed, killed, killed

Masochist
Chauvinist
Altruist
Martyr
Pushed over
Crushed under
Pain and gore

Finished
Destroyed
Unrepentant
Flame no more
Abandoned
Rejected
Vomited

I'm done
Done, done!

GAUDIUM ET VERITAS[1]

_____

[1] Joy and truth.

P A RIS

Paris with you, without you
Long promenades and nothing in sight
Bicycle rides, you laugh the wind off
Muscles and nerves
Air in your nostrils
Breathe me in, if you can:
Never

In love with you, without you
What else did you forget?
Stolen soul, lost direction
Misinterpreted sigh
Forbidden lie
Fight me, if you can:
Loser

Paris and you, without me
Long promenades and stormy nights
Bicycle rides, you fight against the wind
Legs and feet
Air in your nostrils
Exhale me, if you can:
Never

JUBILANT CREATURE

Impure glow detailing lips
embedded in the tropical sun;
Fleeing from melancholic lullabies
his charming voice will rest.

In the brown eyes a light,
showing the way to salvation
to pilgrims caught in a devious act.

A breath of splendour in the docile mouth,
open to welcome dazzling kisses;
The lost island hot flavours
reviving dead cold winters.

Bloodline after bloodline
the seed has passed
through fiery trial,
immortal flame of untamed fire.

A faraway angel, and more than this to spare
the indignant merchant who buys freedom,
no lies to be told
no fear to share.

A voice in the arms of memory
for evermore regretting
the loss of time regained.

Of paradise and hell
those lips will taste once more;
Judge them not for what they say
but for the softness of their miniscule embrace.

The sweet vibration fades
where shadows long to stay.
The joy of angel found
in torrid fire
and melting ground.

The line one has to cross
in silent mourning
of love once lost.

A man or creature
only in dreams revealed;
A dream he is
but—oh—so very real!

Αλφάβητ 🎵

(Alphabet Notes)

A

He dances
Immortalised by sin
La voix retentissante[1]
The eyes wander
Not too far
Just where I am
Bound to contemplate
His little dance of love.

B

Who is he?
He is death
Where is he?
He is in me
When is he?
He is eternal
What is he?
He is snow
How is he?
He is tender

---

[1] The resounding voice.

Why is he?
Because I have made him.

C

Don't talk
Sometimes words are empty
Don't smile
Sometimes you soul is showing
Don't love
Sometimes your love can kill.

D

If I could reach you
I'd tell you my story
If I could kill you
I'd be reborn
If you could see me
You'd be forever.

E

Redundant:
Like you in the crowd
That quickly rejects
Your tears and your plea.
At peace:
Like the frozen ocean
From which you came
To storm my heart away.
Untouched:
Like the sky you forgot
To paint with colours

As marching clouds besiege
Your stone cold heart.

F

I can't stop!
I won't end
This crazy romance
That's all in my head
And blows like sand
Won't break and won't bend
Won't leave nor mend
The broken pieces of hope
Cutting deep to send
Streams of blood into my hands . . .
Forget!

G

Play with me
Lie with me
Sing with me
Jump with me
Run with me
Kill with me
Rhyme with me
Be! Be! Be!

I Love You

I love . . .
Your heart-shaped lips
that softly talk,
whispering in the loud wind
of winters that'll never be,
and falls you can foresee.

I love . . .
Your pretty eyes
hiding the soul
I want to crash;
Your clueless expression
of childish joy
when you look astonished,
embarrassed and coy.

I love . . .
Your smile:
a shot to the heart,
a mesmerising jump
in to the blood pumping system,
that circles and stops
then cuts to the bone.

I love . . .
The intensity
of your pure mind,

so simple yet perfect
truly one of a kind.

And you're one in a million,
and she's nothing but your minion.
We'd die for a chance
to feel slaves to your hand.

But you never look,
never turn your head to see;
you run through the mist
and fail to conceive

That we are in awe
of your perfect soul
I love you, it's true:
your beauty I can't resist.
I love you, it's real:
but you don't exist.

[1] Fate calls the strong ones.

Remembrance

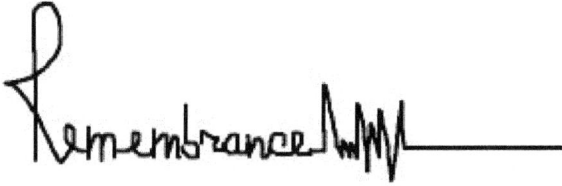

The sand on the far away beach
is red-tinted.
The ground on which I walk
is hot and shallow.
A stray dog over the busy road
has fleas to offer.

When stone becomes sand
the beach gets feet,
to walk across the road
and kick the dying dog down.
So I will cry.

Inside I have the sand
of an hourglass.
Sirens of doom
in the misty morning,
they break the silence
where silence is no more,
and the red-tinted sand
will blow.

I am dust

I sit in my pyjamas all day thinking of you.
You don't even understand my words,
they're collateral to your swinging moods.
How's your heart today?
Any news I should know of?
Oh, I can't live each day in fear
of the latent neck snap,
the rogue assassin shows no hesitation
when life is served on a silver platter.
No, I just don't want to live:
I'm through with this obsession.
Behaving like a fool
and you don't even see it.
When one acts foolishly for you
it means one loves you:
or is it two?

Just thinking for a second:
can you not see my dying shadow?
I'd rather annihilate myself than see you suffer.
But I can only sit and stare,
defying this terrible mess inside my head;
then all that I do is write about it,
while you don't even look at these letters
sounding like murder to your delicate ears.
So . . . Are you bored yet?

I think I'm cursed, I'm sure I am;
it makes no difference so far,
lower the hammer, if you please.
Kill me now and forever,
save yourself from my cancerous love:
do it for the sake of the world.
But remember always this moment,
I could have been your benign drug
and you the junkie.
Instead I'm dust
that blows in all directions,
and you, my love,
have never even known me.

How love dies

Love agonises on a sandy beach
killed by you,
gone for good.
It lies down shattered,
imminent demise in sight . . .
While seagulls laugh hysterically
at this broken heart.

Radiations

These rays are a Molotov bomb:
I wish they'd hit me like you did.
The subatomic particles of your voice
divert my impulse,
detach my suicidal song
from the electromagnetic notes
bombarding vessels in my head.

You'll never say a word,
never speak to me,
so I'll let you know
how much I hate them,
the girls, those impudent girls
showing suddenly at your side.
I file fangs of love
while passion collects dust and germs,
disposing of ductile, microscopic plankton
unnecessary to this cause.

Electrons revive my spirit
only when you exist.
You've been too scarce in your appearance
on this unfunny show;
I'm gagging for your presence
and suffocating,
eating sparkles or nothing at all.
Let me explain all the things that you are,

allow me to decode
the mass of molecules floating in your brain,
attached to this empty hole of mine.

I die, here and forever;
I have to die one more death,
the definitive one.
The atomic version of us
will live on,
though not for all eternity,
exposure to your beauty
so deadly for me now.
Pathetic, revolting,
deprived and insulting,
through space I'll go
ionising the radioactive element,
not caring . . .

And neither will you,
my handsome assassin.
Gamma rays approaching
the unlimited horizon,
will reach my body
devoured by the burning star.
Radioisotopes analysing my remains
as nuclear reactors propel the energy
that heals and destroys.
And so we stand,
apart and divided
in this ultimate nightmare
of a severely contaminated love.

Lost Words

I wrote these words for you,
they're lost in translation,
won't ever be understood.

I cried these tears for an eternity
of bashful attempts
and chocked up feelings;

I asked you these questions
as every night I sit and wonder:
who do you talk to with much ardour?

I scratched these words for you,
they're found in desperation
but won't ever reach you, my love.

Ab imo pectore ♡

_____

[1] From the bottom of my heart.

Different

You believe in god
And I don't
You believe in peace
And I don't
You believe in equality
And I don't
You believe in love
And I don't
You believe in friendship
And I don't
You believe in hope
And I don't
You believe in justice
And I don't
You don't believe in me
And that's the only thing we truly share.

Tomorrow!

Is it possible to drown in sorrow?
With every attempt I unleash a monster
that fails to conquer
your beautiful heart.

Is it necessary to drink the wine
from golden chalices of ancient times?
Delicious taste of old days gone,
the sweet nectar produced by you.

I have dreamt of the day
when brown eyes meet
and soft hands touch
in melancholic peace.

The pain so near
close to unspoken fear,
you far away and distant
fading away in an instant.

What is the word that lingers
on your wet lips tonight?
Please dry my tears at last,
grant me a precious sight.

Is it possible to drown in sorrow?
With every look I reject an offer

that leaves me wounded
every time you say . . . tomorrow!

BEFORE I DIE

I'm writing hell
before I die,
my unheard cry
will haunt you all.

I'm breathing fire,
condemned to suffer
unprecedented pain
of life uncertain.

A place in hell
for me reserved
better than life
so cruelly forced.

I'm writing pain
before I die,
like slaughtered lambs
unheard my cry.

Torn Pictures

This blood stained sheet:
paper butterflies
rubbing against your chest
. . . But you can't feel them.

A voice is broken
while the wind disperses
the ashes of lost souls
. . . But you can't see them.

That blue ribbon
attached to your skin,
pinned down to your throat:
so savagely imposed

on your innocent life,
guilty only of purity:
it still etherises my bad blood
. . . But you don't know it.

That sick joke!
The picture of a fiend,
puking all over the resting place
of one last warrior.

Intact, you walk your path.
Never stopping,

stripping me down
before I die content
in your oblivion.

DIRA NECESSITAS

!

---

[1] The dire necessity.

The Night

So distant
Tonight I live

Only a light
But I don't see it

I look for something:
I'm still waiting . . .

Anxiety getting closer
Tonight
I live

More than a feeling,
More than the impossible one:
This night is impossible

Should it rain
Or should the wind blow;

Should it be daylight
Or still this darkness

Here, right here,
So distant and inaccessible
I live

A WARNING

I am:
scarred, wasted, obliterated,
marked, rejected.

I have:
scars, rubbish, forgetfulness,
marks, relapses.

I feel:
pain, vomit, anger,
recurrence, unresponsiveness.

I give:
sarcasm, intolerance, disappointment,
hopelessness, misunderstanding.

I am not, I don't have, I can't feel,
I won't give:
this putrid soul's for real.

I don't rhyme

I don't rhyme
Nor I mime
I'm never fine
My sun won't shine
I'm not divine
I have no spine
That boy's not mine
I've crossed the line
I taste like lime
I count 'til nine
I'm out of time
So shove this rhyme!

Stop

Don't think:
The piercing eyes
and sweetest smile.
The hurt inside
and pain you hide.

Get him out
of your crazy head;
Erase those dreams
you once had.

Stop

Forget the joy
Make it happen again,
don't be too coy.

Look at the stars,
can't sing out of tune;
Make it your own,
call it safe home.

Stop

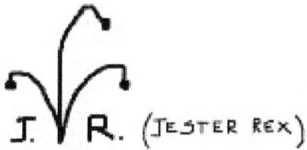

J. R. (JESTER REX)

This is you, looking at me.
Captured by the camera
with plenty to see,
you show not to care,
no indiscretion there.
Posing like a movie star,
but wait a minute:
That's exactly what you are!

The interviews go
back and forth in your life,
I saw you years ago
and never spared a sigh.

Your beauty is uncertain
and mostly perceived as imperfect.
But every now and then
I wonder if you disdain
the compliments from the crowd,
their attention so mundane.

The women at your feet
have nothing but conceit;
favourable suitors attached at your hip
tamed by your smile and gentle whip.

The men they love you too,
though they aren't really meant for you.
A friend in Hollywood,
one romping the neighbourhood,
has taken a fall for you:
the rumours are certainly true.

What part did you once play
in high school, just to get laid?
You're a heartthrob
or so they say;
a bit queer,
but that's okay.

Serial lover of the excessive life,
a marionette of style so fine.
Your eyes are pure
divine your soul,
but men like you
don't stay too long.

You're fake to me,
take no offence.
You're elegant though,
I like your stance.

You're dedicated
to a craft sublime.
Let's face it, darling:
on stage you shine.

And on screen too
your talent grows,

between a chicane
of highs and lows.

Your mother says
she's proud of you,
but all and all
so are we too.

What matters though
is that you're here to stay,
on my screensaver
immortal, real:
a virtual prey.

Final Cut

I'll be cutting pieces off . . . pieces off
Big chunks of flesh . . . my flesh, my flesh
I'll be slicing you up, my heart, black heart
And feeding you to sharks, and hungry cats
I live in the dark and down below
Below the rats
I surface gladly no more
The time forlorn, the clenched fist
I'm razor sharp so there I cut

And cut and cut
If only this was time well spent
I'd puke dissent and swear revenge
But time concocts a plan
The flesh comes off, ignoble device
Sending its double instead
To trick me, or is this a paradox?
Cutting a body mauled by mediocrity
I say:
Who listens? Who can cut this final piece?

And down I go, and go and go
Right where I was a minute ago
I'll be dreaming and screaming
I'll be reading palms and deceiving

I'm good at cutting
I'll be even better
I'm bad at everything
Good deeds are shattered
A slice here
A cut there
My life is over
Ended in despair

DECEPTIO VISUS[1]

---

[1] Optical illusion.

Silver Biting

Biting silver
Silver turns
Turns to gold
Gold will melt
Melt and shine
Shine of glory
Glory of men
Men in despair
Despair of a land
Land in danger
Danger and beauty
Beauty is you
You are silver
Silver is gold
Gold is waiting
Waiting and biting
Biting silver
Relinquish and remember
Amen: you are winning!

The Riddle

Returning
Like a gust of wind
Sweeping away the shadows of darkness,
Through a multitude of eyes
It shatters high in the sky

And it carries on
With the same force
Of powerful, overwhelming waves

And so it goes
Spying on the riptide
Moving through the whirlpool
And the depths of the sea

The dark desire
Releasing strength and violence:
It never gives in

And it comes back
To play hide-and-seek
Heading for Venus
For that's the world
It belongs to

Yet it won't conquer
The ultimate prize

The story truly ends
In chaos and pretence.

It grabs hold of time
And whatever else it can
And this is our dilemma:
Is it demon or just man?

Michelle

Michelle:
In your paradise lost
The ultimate price
You won by chance.
Take a bit of this aching heart
Chew it up and spit it out:
You can

Oh why . . . Why you?
You don't shine
You don't stand out
You are plain
And constantly whine

Michelle:
In your paradise found
I lost my hope.
You took the most precious thing
And now you smile
Your seraphic grin indulges
Over this shattered heart of mine:
You kill

Oh, but why you?
It had to be someone, I know
And it was you,

The beast I cannot fight
The woman who owns time

Michelle:
What paradise is that?
Explain to the phantom child
Your unique fortune

I hate you, I do
It's a black dawn
In my ordinary hell.
When the last bell rings
I wish that I was you

I

I'm afraid
That even the last angel
Has flown away;

I'm afraid
My days are numbered
When all begins to fade;

I'm afraid
That indifference
Will lower the axe
On a troubled life
Running on empty;

I'm afraid
These veins
Won't carry any blood
But wet sand building
Castles destined to shake and fall;

I'm afraid you of many faces
Will reject me one more time
Won't even attempt to guess
The nature of my crimes.

I have little to live for
My life won't matter at all
To the silent human race
Buried underwater
Because I have ceased to exist
Long before I was conceived
By a cursed and withered flower.

My house of horror

In despair
Every hour digs a hole in yesterday
My own head turns to sour
Leaving emptiness right where

There was love, a blessed soul
There it was my life completed
From above, charging off
The call of destiny I've cheated

Come inside my house of horror
Turn the lights on, the show begins
You're a guest of senseless terror
It's impossible to resist
Visit every room and every corner
Clear your head of other sights
Pay a dime to see the plight
Of my house of horror

No regrets
Just the sand of the hourglass on the table
Mystified, terrorised
By the emptiness I left behind

Make it back
To my head
Read the signs spelling danger

Go ahead
Be a man
Don't pretend to be a stranger

Come inside my house of horror
Turn the lights on, the show begins
You're a guest of senseless terror
It's impossible to resist
Visit every room and every corner
Clear your head of other sights
My silly grin welcomes you
To my house of horror

Say a prayer
Don't be scared
Not enough
Time to spare
See me here
Though I'm there
Guided visits . . . everywhere

Come inside my house of horror
Turn the lights on, the show begins
You're a guest of senseless terror
It's impossible to resist
Visit every room and every corner
Clear your head of other sights
Pay a dime to see the plight
Of my house of horror

(This is a song I've written without music. I can't really write music, and the melody comes and goes in my head.)

[1]

IMAGINE
this

Imagine this
Just a bunch of words
With no rhyme or reason
Spat out of a dirty mouth
Mad at the world
And at life itself

Imagine this
Just you and me
You bloody idiots
You scum

Imagine I reached you
And told you the truth
And cried nothing but air
On your welcoming shoulder

Imagine this rage
This cursing aloud
The tumour that grows
And finally shows
Our sorrows and pains

Imagine this
Just a bunch of meaningless words
Spat out of a foul mouth
Mad at the human race
And at life itself.

ABYSMAL MISERY

When infidelity begs for forgiveness
Like a tidal wave surging down the sea,
Of mortality and tedious fierceness
These bones are filled, for all to see.

The lee gunwale in the water:
Where will this heart find peace?
Set sail for revenge,
Then sink the bastards down.

These rules I've made my own
The guilt won't go scot-free;
Virtues mortified and scorned
Perpetually cursing abysmal misery.

Whore

She may be luminous and chic
Yet also talentless, brainless
and quite thick

She thinks she's pretty
Though one can't ignore
Her manly features
And that square jaw

An easy lay
She's always been
For famous lads
The perfect dream

But when one digs
And looks for more
The ugly truth is:
She's a bore

She lacks class
She's bad taste galore
Because this lass
Is just a lowlife whore

---

[1] Pray and work.

2
numbers

Two numbers
Set apart by another
They once got lost
Inside a tunnel

Two numbers
Added up by chance
For better results

On the run
Fugitives without hope
Last seen boarding a train
To nowhere

2 U

Blue eyes
Made of ice
Hooked on lies
Banned from paradise

Juicy lips
Perfect hips
Smile that fits
Into these empty pits

Hell welcomes sand
Planted seeds on desert land
Desires not so grand
Futile and hard to stand

Nothing to lose
This heart overused
Madness and abuse
In your baby blues

And so it ends
This fake romance
Right where it began
Detestable sham.

HARD as STONE

Nothing will make it better.
Lured in and enticed by darkness,
Hoping that light will follow
On the safe shore of despair:
Who's leading you there?

In the touch of a hand
And a frivolous kiss
The spirit descends
Into the depths of the abyss;
Pit your wits against the deceiver
There is more, far more to see
Even for you
While you're away from me

Who art thou?
I hear that voice:
It is mine to keep.
Are you the stranger

Who's come to take me home?
Or just the danger
Of a reoccurring nightmare
That's never gone?

You, the sign
Never shown in vain
Never ready to remain;
A frugal promise
Mortified in a row
Detained and demised
In this obscene vow

Sealed with iron
The truth is shunned;
It cries of solitude
In the long shadow of my past:
'Please, free my spirit
Make it better now,
Make it last!'

Stolen

We sat in the dim of light
The anguish slowly fading
Our pennants fluttering
in the summer breeze

We contemplated and sank
Into this dusty box
Decaying in a memory
Without the solemn comfort
Of tissue paper flowers

VESTIGIA TeRRent

[1]

[1] The footprints frighten me.

Direct Link 2
www.collartrap.com
(aka HELL!)

The end:
Turbid, beautiful, dirty.
Lips and eyes, and ears,
The stench of sexual madness
That vile desire to possess.
He is the end
The grim reaper, the scythe,
The sharpened knife of a guillotine
Stained and reused
For my demise only

He stands
Taller than the tallest mountain,
Brutally smashing my hopes,
Invested with power
Coming straight from hell.
Hell is his voice
Saying 'Kneel down and worship me,
You dirty servant
You slave, you whore!
To me you belong, a soul to abuse
Till I am satisfied.
Then, you shall crawl

Away from my throne,
And I will feast on your heart
The way I always do.'

Hell is his body
Twisting and turning,
Dancing to music and sounds,
To a new beat
To a clear sign.
He came to destroy,
Detonating a bomb
That spread limbs and blood
And left us numb

Damn you,
The fiend, the brute:
The magician!
Terrifying, ambiguous, outrageous,
Smiling happily,
With heart and soul.
Damnation grows
Inside and out;
Survives nothing
Cannot recede nor amend
The die is cast:
The end.

Body Space Time

In your own words:
'Body is the subject.
Space is the distance, the journey.
Time is the duration.'
Body space time
Your body
Invades my space
Begins and ends it
Perpetually

ZOMBIE LOVER

Zombie lover
Perennial crier
Shocking mouth
Feeding terror
Ripping off
Flesh eating bug
Blue as me
I crave
I maim
Lover of mine
Filling my lungs
With poison
Finish me
I have no will
To survive
Zombie lover
Eat me alive!

Impromptu

Our Cartier rings,
the deafening sound of Vegas.
Your cream suit,
the light blue shirt.
My Tadashi dress,
the limo without a driver.
His loud sneeze,
her pollen allergy.
The gazebo in the night,
Elvis on roller skates.
Our room at the Bellagio,
the automatic curtains.
The sumptuous minibar,
your constant hunger.
My vow unheard before,
the sigh of relief.
We'll do it all over again
in Paris, where we belong.

JAMAIS!

Ce sera jamais nous:
jamais!
Ce sera toujours la douleur:
toujours!

Ses yeux noirs me regardent fixement;
ils sont des roches volcaniques
jetées pour me tuer.

Ce n'est pas sa bouche
et ceci n'est pas son sourire.
C'est un imposteur:
le voleur du rêve.

Avant l'aube, il meurt,
il fond la glace et pleure:
'Si seulement je pourrais vous avoir pour un
instant,
je vous donnerais la vie
et la mort,
certitude indissoluble
de notre existence.'

Mais ce sera jamais nous,
ce sera jamais moi:
jamais!

Never!

This will never be us:
never!
It will always be pain:
always!

His black eyes are staring at me;
they are volcanic rocks
thrown to kill me.

It is not his mouth
and this is not his smile.
It is an impostor:
the thief of dreams.

Before dawn, he dies,
he has melted the ice and so he weeps:
'If only I could have you for a moment,
I would give you life and death,
certainty indissoluble
of our existence.'

But this will never be us,
this will never be me:
never!

you look so fine

You look so fine, Dragon Child.
You look so fine . . .

Mercure

Il n'a pas voulu discuter; il ne perd pas son temps dans une conversation futile.

Mercury

He didn't want to argue; he wastes no time in idle talk.

龍 lóng

La lumière dans ses yeux: un faisceau de dards enflammés.

dragon

The light in his eyes: a bundle of flaming darts.

La puissance

Tu me taquines. Je vis dans la souffrance, mon enfant Dragon, et je meurs en peu plus chaque jour sans toi.

Power

You're teasing me. I live in pain, my Dragon Child, and I die a bit more each day without you.

Don de voyance

J'ai été choquée en te voyant dans un costume qui était identique à celui que j'avais choisi pour notre mariage clandestin. Pourrait-il être que c'est vous, mon enfant Dragon, celui qui va tout détruire?

Clairvoyance

I was shocked to see you wearing a suit which was identical to the one I had chosen for our clandestine wedding. Could it be that it is you, my Dragon Child, the one who will destroy everything?

O

Nothing

niente

rien

nichts

nada

niets

ingenting

لاشـــيء

τίποτα

ничего

nic

nihil

AETERNUM VALE

✝ [1]

---

[1] Farewell forever.

Rosaria Trenta is a published author as well as the owner and founder of CanisTrigger Publishing.

She was born in Rome (Italy) and has published several books, including a first collection of poems—entitled *Miei pensieri folli o giulivi* ('My Crazy Joyous Thoughts')—released when she was only sixteen.

Three more books followed: *Occhi intorno a noi* ('Eyes All Around Us'), 1988; *Epifanie* ('Epiphanies'), 1989; *Escerti di vita* ('Excepts from Life'), 1992.

Her creative efforts have won her a string of awards, both in Italy and in the US, including the International Poet of Merit Award in 1994.

The artist's work focuses on the constant search for a place to call home, where peace could eventually be found. She makes an introspective analysis of herself, which finds a safety valve in the written word; this could be interpreted as a sort of cathartic exercise in alleviating painful memories still lingering in the back of her mind.

For Rosaria Trenta words are like pieces of a puzzle which is destined to remain incomplete, as her search for peace and harmony goes on endlessly.

If you have enjoyed reading *Aquilegia ~ Venomous Verses,* you can also buy our previously available title, **Seven–Diary of an Obsession**, by visiting our website at:

www.canistriggerpublishing.com

www.ingramcontent.com/pod-product-compliance
Lightning Source LLC
Chambersburg PA
CBHW060949040426
42445CB00011B/1065